BUDDHISM FOR KIDS

BUDDHISM *for* KIDS

40 ACTIVITIES, MEDITATIONS, AND STORIES FOR EVERYDAY CALM, HAPPINESS, AND AWARENESS

EMILY GRIFFITH BURKE

ILLUSTRATIONS BY APRIL HARTMANN

ROCKRIDGE
PRESS

Interior and Cover Designer: Emma Hall
Art Producer: Hillary Frileck
Editor: Vanessa Ta
Production Editor: Andrew Yackira

Illustrations © 2019 April Hartmann
Author photo courtesy of © Grace Link

ISBN: Print 978-1-64152-397-4
eBook 978-1-64152-398-1
R1

For Purly Squirrel & Mar Malade.
WITH IMMENSE GRATITUDE TO THE CHILDREN
AND CAREGIVERS OF THE MINDFUL FAMILIES OF
DURHAM AND THE RALEIGH KADAMPA CENTER.

Contents

CHAPTER 3: NIGHT 54

A Note to Caregivers

By picking up this book you have taken a wonderful step toward sharing the Dharma, or the teachings of the Buddha, with the children in your life. I have found in my time working with children that they have a natural curiosity about the way things are—the true nature of things. And when that curiosity is nurtured and encouraged, they arrive at their own Truths.

Just recently I was teaching a class about the golden rule (corresponding to the adult topic of karma), and one of my young students shared their own interpretation of this teaching. They said, "If someone is not nice to you, it does not mean you should not be nice to them." I was so taken that this young student expanded the idea of treating others as you would like to be treated to include such a nuanced understanding of reciprocity. With only a simple introduction to the golden rule, this student's curiosity carried them to the wisdom they already held in their heart.

This book is designed to cultivate natural curiosity in a way that opens children's minds to a Buddhist way of interacting with the world. Through hearing the stories, practicing the meditations, and playing through the activities outlined in this book, children will explore the Dharma and see how it relates to their moment-to-moment experience. Such explorations will help cultivate mindfulness, calm, healthy relationships, empathy, and compassion.

Children may have questions while working through the activities in this book, and I encourage you to reflect questions back to them in an open-ended way. What do they think about the question? How does it feel for them to ask it? Do they notice a pull toward any specific ideas or words? Often the mere act of asking a question indicates a deeper understanding hiding just beneath the surface. With a little investigation, a child's own realization of the Truth can be revealed.

I'd like to note that this is not a book on Buddhist philosophy, nor an instructional manual that needs to be followed in a strict manner. It also is not affiliated with one specific school of Buddhism, but instead draws inspiration and concepts from many traditions.

The activities in this book are designed to be fun and easy ways for children to engage with and practice the Dharma at their own level. It is most suitable for children at the preschool level or older. Younger children can use this book with help from an adult, and older kids can use it independently as they learn to read and follow directions on their own.

Finally, as a caregiver guiding a child along their spiritual path, know that the Buddha instructed us to "come and see for ourselves"; the Buddha taught that each practitioner must explore and experience the Dharma themselves to realize its Truth. May these activities provide spiritual nourishment to both you and your child as you walk the path.

Introduction

When I was growing up, I used to dream of a grassy, sunny meadow in the middle of the forest. On some nights, I dreamt I was playing games in the grass with the insects and plants all around me. On other nights, I dreamt I was simply walking around and admiring the beautiful clearing. Sometimes my friends were with me in these dreams; sometimes I was sitting quietly by myself. In the morning, I would wake up from my dream feeling refreshed, calm, and present.

Something about the meadow and the activities I would do there opened my heart to a feeling of connection with the world, and this connection led me to feel peace. I've created this book as a guide for children, like you, to learn activities that help grow such feelings of connection and peace. I learned later in life that such loving activities can be described as *Buddhist*, and I began to practice and teach Buddhism to adults and children.

Buddhism is a religion, philosophy, and spiritual path. Buddhism began in India about 2,500 years ago when a man named Siddhartha Gautama learned the way to end the experience of human suffering. When he awakened to this realization, or became *enlightened*, he became the Buddha, and began to teach what he learned.

The Buddha's teachings, or the *Dharma*, offer us many different approaches to inner peace. Some teach us how to feel calm and centered. Others teach us how to be more aware of what is happening around and within us. Still others teach us how to respond when we feel different emotions. We can use different teachings depending on what we need in each moment.

The activities in this book are designed to teach you different parts of the Dharma, showing you ways to grow your inner peace in different situations. The book is divided into three sections: morning, day, and night. Since we have different energy levels depending on the time of day, the activities are grouped based on the time for which they are best suited. The morning activities will help you feel energized and focused for the day ahead. The day activities will help you find balance and awareness. The night activities will help you feel calm and tranquil as you settle down for sleep.

In the following pages you'll find meditations, stories, games, and projects. Meditations will be labeled with a ⬤. Stories will be labeled with a ⬤. Games and projects are considered activities, labeled with a ⬤.

If you're younger, you and your caregiver can decide together what type of activity is right for each moment and play through them together. As you get older, you can use this book independently to select the activity that feels right for you. And remember, every day is different, so activities can be repeated again and again over time. You may even find that a particular activity makes you feel so peaceful and joyful that you want to do it every day.

One last thing to keep in mind is that although these activities are based on Buddhist teachings, they can be enjoyed by anyone. Even if you practice something other than Buddhism, you can use these activities to help grow your inner experience of joy, mindfulness, and peace.

Now, onward to the meadow.

Chapter 1

MORNING

Good morning, and welcome to the day! Morning is a special time when we transition our bodies and minds from sleep to wakefulness. We might still feel sleepy from the night, or we might feel full of energy and ready to move right away. No matter how we tend to feel in the morning, as each day is different, it is important that we set a tone of kindness and mindfulness for the day ahead. If the day is like a house, the morning is like the foundation that the house is built on, so we want to make sure the foundation is strong.

In the morning, it can be helpful to practice feeling into our bodies and seeing if they are asking us for something, like water, food, movement, or a walk outside. We might also check in with our minds and ask ourselves how we are feeling. When we practice tuning into our bodies and minds in the morning, we can better understand what we need and what will be our practices for the day. We can then choose the five- to fifteen-minute activities in this chapter that are right for us today. And remember, it can be helpful to repeat the same activities multiple times until you feel ready to move on.

The Brave Buddha Bird

This is a retelling of a story from the Jataka Tales. The Jataka Tales are an ancient collection of imaginative stories about the Buddha as both a human and an animal.

Once upon a time, before the Buddha was born as a human, he was born as a little parrot in a great forest full of animals. One day, a storm was stirring overhead. Lightning flashed, thunder clapped, and suddenly—CRACK—a tree was struck by lightning and burst into flames!

"Fire! Fire!" shouted the animals fearfully. "We must get to the river." The little parrot joined the fleeing animals as they ran toward the river. As he flew overhead, he noticed that many animals were trapped by the fire and unable to escape.

Once at the river, he turned to the other animals and said, "Many of our friends are trapped in the forest. We have to go back and help them." But the other animals shook their heads. "It is too dangerous," they said. "And you are just a little bird. How could you possibly help?" The parrot paused, staring out over the river, when he had an idea.

With great speed, the little parrot dived into the river, scooping up water in his wings. He called upon his courage as he flew straight back into the flames, flapping his wings and shaking droplets of water into the fire. The little parrot returned to the river, coughing from the smoke. Without hesitation he dived down again, gathering more water into his wings and returning to the fire. Back and forth the little bird flew, carrying the small bit of water he could and shaking it onto the flames.

Overhead, a jolly group of gods and goddesses were enjoying a great feast in the clouds when one goddess noticed the little parrot struggling against the great fire. Intrigued by the little bird's bravery, the goddess transformed herself into an eagle and flew down to meet the parrot. "Little one, you cannot possibly put out such a large fire with mere drops of water. Go back to the river and save yourself."

"I will not go back," cried the little bird between coughs. "Many more animals are suffering, trapped by the flames. I will not rest until they are all free." The eagle-goddess looked down and saw the animals still trapped in the forest, in pain and fear, surrounded by fire, and she looked at the little bird working tirelessly to save them.

The eagle-goddess' heart softened and she was overcome with compassion. She began to cry. Miraculously, as her tears fell they swelled into sparkling, golden streams of rain. The little parrot looked on as the tears of the crying eagle-goddess put out the great flames.

The animals below looked up at the little parrot with gratitude and began to cheer. The eagle-goddess bowed to the little bird as she wiped away the last of her tears, and thanked him for inspiring such compassion.

NO MATTER HOW SMALL, A BEING WITH A HEART OF COMPASSION CAN HAVE A GREAT EFFECT ON THE WORLD.

Breathing Our Way Awake

Soon after you wake up from your night's sleep, sit up on your bed, chair, floor, or cushion. Sit in a position that feels comfortable. You might cross your legs, cross one leg with the other outstretched, stretch out both legs in front of you, or sit on your heels. Close your eyes and rest your hands on your legs.

Now, count three slow *deep breaths*, in through your nose, and out through your nose. Fill your lungs fully as you breathe in, and push all the air out as you breathe out. After you count three deep breaths through your nose, count three *arm-raise breaths* to wake up your body: Breathe in through your nose and stretch your arms up over your head, reaching for the ceiling like an elephant raising its trunk. Then, breathe out through your mouth as you float your arms back down.

After you count three *arm-raise breaths*, open your eyes and take three *lion's breaths*: Breathe in through your nose and out through your mouth, sticking out your tongue and making an "ah" sound as you breathe out. As you breathe out, imagine that you are a mighty lion, roaring into wakefulness.

You can now slowly open your eyes. Keeping your body still, look around the room and see what you notice. You might name the colors of the objects you see, or think about the shapes. Pick one object in the room and focus your eyes on it as you count three final *deep breaths* in and out through your nose. Repeat this breathing meditation until you feel energized and focused. Welcome to awake!

Step-by-Step Walking Meditation

Practice this walking meditation when your body wants to move in the morning, or when you feel sleepy and want to wake up.

Choose a location, inside or outside, with plenty of open space for walking around. You might take off your shoes and walk barefoot. If practicing with multiple people, begin with everyone standing in a circle. If practicing on your own, pick a place as your starting location for walking in a circle.

Begin by grounding your feet into the floor beneath you. What do you notice about how your feet feel? Can you feel the pressure of the floor? What is its texture? Is it hot or cold? You might wiggle your toes and see how that feels.

Next, slowly shift your weight to your left side and lift up your right foot like a flamingo. Hold your balance for just a moment, and then slowly lower your right foot back down. How do your legs and feet feel? Repeat by shifting your weight to the right and lifting your left foot. Once you've lowered it back down, again notice any feelings in your legs and feet.

Choose the direction you'd like to walk in, and turn your body to face that direction. When you're ready, breathe in as you take your first slow step, noticing how you shift your weight, lift, and touch your foot back down to the ground. Continue taking slow, small steps around in a large circle, noticing how it feels to walk.

When you're back to your starting position, walk around in the same circle again, but walk more quickly and less mindfully. When you get back to your starting location again, return to slow, mindful steps. Repeat this walking meditation until you feel a sense of ease and balance in your body and mind.

Greet the Trees ✎

Do you ever stop and notice trees? These magnificent plants are all around us and do so much to support life, including providing the air we breathe. The Buddha taught that we are interconnected with other living beings and nature, including trees. This activity helps us connect with trees, a category of living beings that we often forget to think about.

Soon after waking up, prepare to take a walk outside. Younger children should go for a walk with a caregiver, and older kids can get permission to walk on their own. You might choose to walk barefoot if it is safe for your feet and your caregiver says it's OK. Walk outside slowly, feeling the ground beneath your feet. You might practice the *Step-by-Step Walking Meditation* (page 6) as you first walk outside.

Slowly approach a tree. If there is not a tree near your home, you can instead approach a bush or plant. When you are close enough to the tree, take a moment to greet it. You might say hello, wave, or bow. It may feel a little silly at first to greet a tree in this way, and that's OK. It can be fun to try new ways of interacting with the world.

Next, take in the tree using your senses. The five senses are seeing, touching, hearing, smelling, and tasting. It's not a good idea to taste objects that live outside, as they might be harmful, so practice using the other senses. What does the tree look like? Observe its beautiful, complex patterns. Look at the bark and the branches. Are there leaves? Pine needles? Can you see any roots sticking up from the ground?

Next practice touching the tree. What does it feel like? You might close your eyes as you touch the tree in order to focus your attention on touch. Do the different parts of the tree feel similar to or different from to each other? Try tracing the bark with your fingers and see where the lines take you.

Now try listening to the tree. Can you hear the leaves rustling in the wind? Maybe an animal scurrying around the branches? Something else? You might even hear the tree telling you a secret!

Finally, try smelling the tree, with your eyes closed. Does the smell remind you of anything? What does it feel like to take in the tree's scent?

Take a few moments to appreciate all the gifts that trees offer us: oxygen, timber, shade, beauty . . . can you think of anything else that trees do to support life? Bow to the tree in gratitude for its offerings, and tell it "thank you" for all that it does to support life.

The Buddha and the Blind ⓘ

This story is adapted from an Indian parable; it is a classic story that helps explain a big idea.

Once upon a time, a group of villagers came to the Buddha hoping he would settle a disagreement. Half of the group said, "The way to peace is through sitting meditation." The other half of the group said, "No, the way to peace is through walking meditation."

"Tell us who is right," they shouted. The Buddha nodded, and asked them to gather all the people in the village who were born blind, unable to see, and ask if they could help them solve the problem. The villagers agreed and returned with five blind people who had offered to help.

The Buddha thanked these blind people for their help and brought them over to an elephant. He took a blind woman by the hand and walked her over to the elephant's head. The Buddha asked her to reach out and feel what was in front of her, saying, "This right here, is an elephant."

He then took the hands of a blind man and walked him over to the elephant's leg, asking him to feel what was in front of him and saying, "This right here, is an elephant."

The Buddha showed the rest of the blind helpers the elephant's tail, belly, and tusks. He then said to them all, "Please describe to me what an elephant is like."

The first woman, who had felt the elephant's head, said, "An elephant is like a pot." The second man, who had felt the elephant's leg, said, "No, no, an elephant is like

a pillar." The other blind helpers began to argue, "No, it's not, an elephant is like a brush!" "A wall!" "A hammer!"

The villagers who had been arguing about the right way to peace watched on as the blind helpers argued about what an elephant is. One villager stepped forward and said, "Here, you are all right. See, you have each touched a different part of the whole elephant." And they walked the blind helpers over to the elephant to touch along the whole elephant body.

The blind helpers then understood, and the villagers looked to the Buddha as they exclaimed, "Oh!"

"You are all correct," said the Buddha. "Just as each of our helpers has been correct in describing a part of the whole elephant, you have each touched a different part of the path to peace."

THERE IS NO ONE RIGHT WAY TO LOOK AT SOMETHING. EVERY PERSPECTIVE IS ONE PIECE OF THE WHOLE TRUTH.

Intention Bench

An *intention* is something that we focus on and aim for with our thoughts, words, and actions. Intentions are similar to goals, but goals focus on *what* we plan to do, and intentions focus on *how* we want to do it. For example, you might have a goal to finish cleaning your room today; an intention could be to practice being mindful while you clean it.

It is useful to set intentions because it can help set a positive tone for the day. In a day without an intention, you might clean your room but feel bad while doing it. In a day with an intention to be mindful, you might clean your room and also enjoy the process. Setting an intention is like playing your favorite song in the background while you work on a project; it can make you feel happy and excited to live out your day.

This activity will help you to choose an intention for the day by reflecting and drawing. Divide a piece of paper into three sections.

1. Intentions are often based on *values*, or personal traits and actions that you find most important in life. Some examples of Buddhist values are kindness, compassion, honesty, empathy, mindfulness, acceptance, sincerity, and generosity. Choose one value that is important to you and write it down or draw a picture representing it in the first section.

2. In the second section, draw a picture of an activity you plan to do today.

3. In the last section, draw an intention that you can focus on to bring your value to today's activity. Here are some examples:

   - I choose the *value* of generosity today, and I plan to go play at the park. I *intend* to practice sharing with others while I am playing at the park.

   - I choose the *value* of kindness today, and I plan to help my parent with chores around the house. I *intend* to use kind words and have a kind attitude while I help my parent.

   - I choose the *value* of honesty today, and I plan to go to school. I *intend* to only speak the truth to my teachers and friends while at school.

Once you have chosen your intention for the day, find a chair, bench, cushion, or spot on the floor to sit for a few moments; this is your *intention bench*. Close your eyes, and slowly say your intention out loud to yourself three times. Then, open your eyes and notice how you feel. You are ready to start your day with intention!

As you go about your day with your intention, check in with yourself three separate times and ask, "Have I been practicing my intention?" If you have, that's great! If you haven't, then the check-in can help you remember your intention. Tomorrow you can decide if you'd like to practice more with today's intention or set a new one.

The Monkey Queen and the Water Demon

This is a retelling of a story from the Jataka Tales. The Jataka Tales are an ancient collection of imaginative stories about the Buddha as both a human and an animal.

Once upon a time before the Buddha was born as a human, he was born as a Monkey Queen to a family of 80,000 monkeys. The Monkey Queen was wise and kind, and watched over her monkey family with love.

In the forest where the monkey family lived, there also lived Water Demons, who dwelled in the rivers and gobbled up any creature that entered the water. The Monkey Queen knew of the Water Demons, so she warned her family to never go for a drink or swim in unknown water until the Monkey Queen could inspect it for demons. The monkey family had great trust in their leader, so they always waited for the Monkey Queen before swimming or drinking.

One day, the 80,000 monkeys came across a lovely river they had never visited before. Although they were hot and thirsty, they decided to wait for the Monkey Queen before entering the river. The Monkey Queen arrived and was grateful to see her family had waited. She approached the river carefully and noticed some footprints going toward the river. She looked for other footprints leaving the river, but did not see any.

"My family, I see footprints entering the river but not leaving it; the animals that have swam and drank here before never left. I'm afraid in this river lives a Water Demon!" The 80,000 monkeys gasped.

"But what are we to do, Monkey Queen? We have been walking all day and are so thirsty."

Suddenly, a large wave grew out of the river, and a giant green demon with large, sharp teeth emerged from the water. "Come into the river to quench your thirst," said the Water Demon.

"Do not listen to him!" exclaimed the Monkey Queen to her family. She turned to the Water Demon, "I know of your plan to lure animals into the water and then eat them for lunch, and you will not touch my family. But, we *will* enjoy drinking from this beautiful river." The Water Demon looked perplexed.

The wise Monkey Queen leaped into a nearby tree and began pulling bamboo sticks from the forest, handing them out to the 80,000 monkeys. "We shall use these as straws to drink from the river," exclaimed the queen.

The monkeys cheered and began to sip from the bamboo straws, with a safe distance from the Water Demon. Soon they stopped, confused, and the Water Demon began to laugh. "Ha ha ha! The Monkey Queen is so unwise that she did not know the bamboo sticks have knots in them. You will not be able to drink from my river."

The Monkey Queen bowed her head and placed her hands in prayer position. Then, with a burst of insight, she brought a bamboo stick to her mouth and blew through it with one quick breath. Her breath moved through the bamboo like a gust of wind, and the inside was cleared of the knots. She dipped her bamboo stick in the river, and began to drink the cool water. The other 80,000 monkeys also blew into their bamboo sticks, and cheered as they, too, began to drink from the river through their bamboo straws.

The Water Demon pouted and turned to reenter his home in the water, when the Monkey Queen swung by from a vine overhead, and kindly handed the Water Demon his very own bamboo drinking straw. The Water Demon chuckled in gratitude as he sunk back down deep beneath the water.

HAVE TRUST IN THOSE WHO ARE WISE.

CREATIVE SOLUTIONS ARE ALWAYS AVAILABLE IN TIMES OF NEED.

Mind Mapping

Reflection: Turn your attention inward to your mind. Listen to any thoughts that arise and observe what they feel like or sound like. Ask yourself the following questions:

- Do your thoughts have different voices or tones?
- Are there personalities or character traits that you notice in your thoughts?
- Are there multiple characters in your thoughts, or just one?
- How loud are your thoughts? Are some louder than others?
- Do your thoughts talk to each other? For example, you might have one thought that says, "I want to go back to bed," and another thought that says, "But I'm excited to play with my friends today." How do these different mind-characters talk with each other?
- Imagine what each character might look like. How might they dress? What facial expressions do they make?

Imagine the characters of all your thoughts interacting in a room together. Remember that everyone is welcome and allowed to be there.

Activity: Draw a large circle on a sheet of paper. This circle represents your mind in this moment. Divide the circle into different-sized sections like a pizza. Each section will hold one of the characters of your mind. The mind-voices that sound loudest right now can live in the larger sections, and the more quiet voices can live in the smaller sections. In each section, draw what you imagine the character looks like. Pay special attention to their facial expressions. You can name them if you want.

When you've finished creating your mind map, take a look at the finished product. What do you notice about the different characters of your mind? Does your map represent how you feel right now?

Remember that the characters of your mind will not look the same way, or be as loud or quiet as they are now forever. Everything changes, and each day is different. You can repeat this activity when your mood has changed and observe how your mind characters sound and look different as well. Just as our feelings and thoughts are always changing, so our mind maps are always changing.

Morning Metta

Metta means loving-kindness in an ancient language called Pali. Loving-kindness is a feeling of love, friendliness, and interest toward others. You might have felt metta before when you've cheered on a friend, welcomed someone new to your school, or hugged your parent. Metta means you want others to be happy. Practice this meditation to grow the feeling of metta in your heart as you start your day.

Sit on a chair, the floor, or a cushion. Position your body so that you are comfortable. You might cross your legs, cross one leg, stretch out your legs in front of you, or sit on your knees. Place both of your hands over your heart and close your eyes. If it feels hard to sit still like this, you can rock back and forth or slowly move your upper body around in a circle.

Keeping your hands on your heart, think of someone you love very much. It might be a parent or caregiver, a sibling, another family member, a friend, neighbor, or pet. Imagine that this being is sitting in front of you, and see how you feel. Do you feel warm? Do you want to smile? Do you feel happy? Safe? Cared for?

Continue to imagine this being is sitting with you, and focus on their face. Now, imagine them filling with joy and smiling at you with happiness. Notice how you feel as you look at their smiling face and feel their happiness. How does your heart feel?

Finally, say, "Thank you. I love you. May you be happy" to this being. You can say this out loud or to yourself. Repeat these words three times or more, and continue to imagine them sitting in front of you. Close this meditation by noticing the feelings in your heart one last time, bringing your hands together in prayer position, and bowing your head down to the floor.

You can carry this feeling of metta with you throughout the day. If you face a challenge or have a hard time at any point, you can remember the image of someone you care about smiling at you and feel the metta in your heart.

Alien the Great Steps into the Precepts

Note: This activity is best done in a group of three or more people.Use this activity to help you think about what is right and what is wrong as you start your day.

In Buddhism, the *precepts* are guidelines for our speech and actions. They help us determine if the things we say and do are helpful or harmful. The five precepts are:

1. Be kind; do not cause harm to other beings.

2. Be generous; do not steal.

3. Be a wholesome friend; do not make others uncomfortable.

4. Tell the truth; do not lie.

5. Feed your body healthy foods and drinks; do not feed your body harmful things.

In this activity, someone will play the role of an alien visiting Earth from space, and others will play the role of Earth teachers. Decide together who will play each role, and act out the scenario below.

Alien the Great from space discovered the planet Earth and has come for a visit to learn about humans. Alien the Great is greeted by Earth teachers, who welcome the visitor and ask what he would like to learn. Alien the Great says, "What are your guidelines for how to be a good human? How do you know what is right and what is wrong?" The Earth teachers decide to use the Buddhist precepts as a guide to answer Alien the Great's questions.

Earth teachers, choose one precept to explain to Alien the Great. You might want to act out situations that show what to do and what not to do. Alien the Great, be sure to ask questions; remember, you are a visitor from space and don't know about life on Earth. You need to know how to be a good earthling during your stay on planet Earth.

When you've finished explaining a precept, you might switch roles and explain another precept to a new Alien the Great. And, remember, the precepts come up in many different situations, so you can explain them in many different ways. Thanks for helping Alien the Great!

Chapter 2

DAY

Welcome to the daytime chapter. Day tends to be a more active time when we experience a range of situations and emotions. We often spend time with others as well, playing games or working on projects in groups. We may spend more time outside during the day, and want to find activities we can do outside with our friends. After a more active day it is often common that we take a break for a rest, perhaps a nap as well. This chapter offers us stories, meditations, and activities that are well suited to the many different types of encounters we face during the day. These pages also provide good reminders of the values we want to focus on while interacting with others during the day, things like honesty, managing anger, kindness, and belonging.

I Belong, You Belong

The Buddha was a teacher who taught everyone. He did not only teach very smart people, nor did he only teach very rich people. He taught the rich and the poor, the monks and the laypeople, men, women, and all genders, elders, and children. The Buddha taught that all beings belong in the circle of life, and that including everyone is important.

Practice this meditation with one or more friends.

Sit in a circle or across from one another. Begin by taking three deep breaths together. Breathe in through the nose and out through the mouth. Then, close your eyes and think about what it means to belong. How does it feel when you belong? Have you ever been excluded from something? How did that feel?

When you've finished reflecting, open your eyes and look around until everyone else has opened their eyes, too.

Then, go around the circle and take turns saying out loud, "I belong, you belong." When you say "you belong," point and bow to one person in the circle to signal that it is their turn. That person will then repeat "I belong, you belong" and point and bow to another member of the circle.

Be mindful of making sure everyone gets a turn to feel included with a point and bow and the chance to say the phrase. Once everyone has had several turns to say the phrase out loud, close the meditation by saying together, "we all belong" and bowing to one another. Finally, go around the circle and give everyone the chance to share how this group meditation felt.

Beginner's Mind

In Buddhism, having a *beginner's mind* is considered helpful and wise. When we think we are advanced or know everything, meditation actually becomes a lot harder. In this meditation you will reflect on the wonderful aspects of being a beginner.

This meditation can be done while sitting, or while mindfully walking. If you need a reminder, you can revisit *Breathing Our Way Awake* (page 5) or *Step-by-Step Walking Meditation* (page 6). Choose which type of meditation feels best for your body and mind, and find a comfortable seated position or walking rhythm.

As you settle in, take a few moments to notice what is happening in your mind. Are there thoughts? Attitudes? Feelings? Notice how you feel about the meditation you are doing. Are you excited? Nervous? Content? Frightened? Encouraged?

Now, think about what it means to be a beginner. When have you been a beginner at something? How did it feel? Do you feel like a beginner in your meditation practice? What is that like?

Sometimes we might think being a beginner is a bad thing, because we do not feel skilled at an activity. But the Buddha taught that the mind of a beginner is very powerful. Beginners are often excited about their activity, open to learning new skills and ways of doing things, and do not assume they know the answer.

Focus your mind on what it feels like to be excited about learning something new. How does it feel to be eager to learn a new skill or activity?

Next, focus your mind on how it feels to be open to learning new things. You might think about moments when you pay careful attention to a teacher.

Finally, focus your mind on what it is like to not know the answer to something, This might feel frustrating at first, but think about it a little bit more. When we think we know the answers, we might miss the opportunity to learn a new perspective or Truth.

Close this meditation by saying aloud the phrase "beginner's mind" three times and smiling as you bow.

Shina and the Samurai

This story is adapted from a Zen Buddhist parable; it is a classic story that helps explain a big idea.

Once, long ago, there was a little old nun named Shina who was very wise. Shina spent most of her days deep in meditation, cultivating a kind heart and the wisdom to know how to best teach her visitors who came to learn from her.

One day, Shina was approached by a menacing samurai. The samurai was tall and strong, and carried two sharp swords. He was covered in armor and looked ready to fight at any time. Shina sat calmly on her cushion as she greeted the stranger.

"Old nun, teach me about the roots of war and peace. I need to know. Tell me or I will fight you!"

Shina frowned at the warrior and said, "Teach *you*? You expect me to teach you about war and peace? You are not worthy of my wisdom. You are dirty, smelly, and don't know anything! A disgrace to all samurai."

The samurai grew red with fury and pulled out his swords, ready to attack little old Shina. "You dare insult me, old lady?"

Shina smiled calmly and lifted a finger, "Ah, and there, my friend, you have found the root of war."

The samurai paused, lowering his swords. "You mean . . . ?"

"Anger, like the anger you just felt and were about to act on, is what leads to violence." said Shina humbly. The samurai took a deep breath, then looked Shina in the eye.

"I was going to attack you. You risked your life to teach me the Truth." The samurai's heart softened, and his eyes filled with tears of gratitude.

Shina nodded as she said kindly, "Ah, and there, my friend, you have found the root of peace."

She offered the warrior a hug as he cried with knowing this new wisdom. The samurai decided to give up his life of fighting and join Shina in the monastery to learn meditation and teach others of the danger of anger and the bliss of gratitude.

CONFLICT AND HARM COME FROM ANGER. PEACE COMES FROM GRATITUDE AND SELFLESSNESS.

The Plate of Gold

This is a retelling of a story from the Jataka Tales. The Jataka Tales are an ancient collection of imaginative stories about the Buddha as both a human and an animal.

Once upon a time there were two salesmen, Hriyaan and Mamun, who would travel from village to village selling their wares. Hriyaan was a greedy man who was cheap with his customers. Mamun was honest, trustworthy, and generous.

One day the two salesmen arrived at a village and split up to sell their wares. Hriyaan walked up a street pushing his cart and calling out, "Pots and pans! Jewelry and bands!" Inside a small hut, a little girl named Priya heard Hriyaan's shouts and rushed over to her grandmother.

"Oh, Grandmother! A salesman is in town and says he has jewelry. Please, could I buy a simple bracelet from him?"

Grandmother looked at the little girl sadly. "My dear, I would love to buy you a bracelet, but you know we are poor and have nothing to trade with the salesman."

Priya noticed a dirty old plate gathering dust on a shelf in the corner. "What about this old plate, Grandmother? Could we try to trade that?" Grandmother agreed, and she and Priya went out to the street to offer the old plate to Hriyaan.

"Please sir, my granddaughter would be delighted to have one of your fine bracelets. Might you accept this old plate in exchange?" Hriyaan took the plate from Grandmother and inspected it. He scratched the bottom of the plate, and behold! It was made of pure gold.

Rather than inform the old lady of his discovery, greedy old Hriyaan devised a deceptive plan. "This plate is worth nothing," he lied to Grandmother. "It is not even worth my simplest bracelet." He set down the plate and strode away, secretly planning to return later and trade only a rupee for the plate.

Priya and Grandmother were saddened, but soon they saw Mamun pushing his cart up the street. "Oh, Grandmother, perhaps *this* salesman will accept our old plate for a bracelet."

Mamun greeted the two ladies kindly and began to inspect the plate. With awe he, too, realized that the plate was made of pure gold. "My friend," he said to Grandmother. "This plate is made of pure gold. I will trade you all of my wares and all of my money, save but eight coins for the ferry, in exchange for this plate. Might you accept this humble offer?"

Priya gasped, and Grandmother took Mamun's hand, saying, "Thank you, kind salesman, for your honesty. I accept your generous offer." And so Mamun handed over his entire cart of wares and all of his money save but eight coins, and he went on his way to the ferry to go sell the plate of gold in the city. Grandmother and Priya rejoiced in their good fortune.

Before long, Hriyaan returned to Grandmother and Priya, saying, "I've thought about it and, out of the kindness of my heart, I'll give you a rupee for your worthless old plate."

"Ah, but the plate is no longer mine," replied Grandmother. "You see, it turns out it was made of gold. I have sold it to another salesman for a generous exchange, and he now makes his way to the city with it."

"Noooo!" shouted Hriyaan with anger, and he took off running to the river. "Mamun," he bellowed from the river's shore. "That plate is mine. Come back!"

Mamun looked back from the boat. "My dear Hriyaan, it would have been yours had you been more honest."

And with that, Mamun continued on his way, and Hriyaan was left in a fitful rage of regret.

IN THE END, HONESTY AND GENEROSITY WILL TAKE YOU FURTHER THAN LIES AND DECEPTION.

Random Act of Kindness

What does it mean to be kind to others? The Buddha taught that *metta*, or loving-kindness, means being interested in, friendly toward, and generous with others. This activity will allow you to practice metta through a random act of kindness toward a stranger or someone you know.

Begin by taking a few moments to think about kindness. How does it feel when someone is kind to you? What types of actions do you consider kind? How does it feel when you are kind to others?

Next, set an intention to be on the lookout for someone who might need a random act of kindness. It could be someone you know well such as a caregiver, sibling, or friend. Or it could be someone you don't know as well such as a bus driver, neighbor, or store clerk.

Continue on with your day until you come across someone who you think needs some kindness. What might help them to feel good? You might compliment them on their clothing or smile. You might offer them a small gift such as a card or flower. Or you might offer to help someone with a task they are trying to complete.

As you perform your act of kindness, notice how your heart feels. What does it feel like to give your time and energy to others?

If you want to do this activity but do not get the chance to practice with a human, you might do a random act of kindness for the Earth or for an animal by giving your pet a treat or spending some time petting them. You also might feed the birds or pick up garbage outside. Finally, you can offer a random act of kindness to someone you don't know by donating your toys to a charity or volunteering. An act of kindness is never wasted; its effects ripple out and affect others both in ways we can see and ways we cannot see.

The Buddha and the Elephant 🔊

This story is adapted from Buddhist mythology passed down from Buddhist scriptures.

It is said that the Buddha had two cousins, Devadatta and Ananda. Devadatta was very jealous of the Buddha, whereas Ananda was very loyal and trusting.

Devadatta was angry because he wanted to be admired and loved as was the Buddha. Thus he was always looking for ways to harm the Buddha and replace him. One day, Devadatta learned that the Buddha was coming to visit his village. The jealous Devadatta schemed up a sinister plot. He planned to trample the Buddha with Nalagiri the elephant.

The Buddha approached the town with his followers, and Devadatta began to beat poor Nalagiri with sticks. Nalagiri trampled about in anger and pain, and Devadatta continued to hit and yell at her. When Devadatta saw the Buddha walking toward him, he opened the gate, releasing the enraged elephant in the Buddha's direction.

The angry and hurt Nalagiri charged toward the Buddha and his followers at full speed. The frightened followers jumped out of the way, calling to Buddha to get to safety. But Ananda stayed by his side in complete trust, and the Buddha stayed perfectly still.

The Buddha looked the charging elephant in the eyes and called upon the deepest loving-kindness of his heart. He knew that there must be a reason Nalagiri acted in this way and that she was suffering.

Buddha continued to radiate the purest love and compassion toward Nalagiri, and gradually, the animal slowed. The Buddha smiled humbly at the elephant with kindness and understanding, saying, "Hello, Nalagiri. Come, my friend."

The elephant looked at the Buddha, and her anger and pain faded. Nalagiri bowed and knelt down before the great spiritual teacher, and Buddha stroked the tamed animal's ears. Devadatta's misguided plan was foiled, and the crowd cheered for the Buddha's boundless heart.

> NOTE: Recall that this is only a story and not recommended behavior around animals, especially large wild animals.

DO NOT UNDERESTIMATE THE POWER OF LOVE AND COMPASSION.

Silent Leader Walking Meditation

This is a silent walking meditation for two or more people. You can practice this meditation outside, or inside in a large open space.

Begin this meditation by choosing one person to start as the silent leader. Everyone will take turns being the silent leader, so don't worry too much about who goes first. Line up facing the same way, with the silent leader in the front.

When everyone is ready, the silent leader can begin with a slow walking meditation, and everyone behind them in line will follow. The silent leader can then begin to change the style of walking: they might start taking very big steps, or very small steps. They might flap their arms like chicken wings, or add a dance move. They might hop or squat with each step. Or they might even decide to crawl on the floor.

As the silent leader changes the style of walking, everyone behind them in line will copy the movements of the silent leader. After several minutes, the silent leader will clap their hands together once and then move to the back of the line. The next person in line is now the silent leader.

Continue this community walking meditation until everyone has had a chance to be the silent leader at least once. At the end of this meditation, take a few minutes to notice how it feels to be a part of the line and to take your turn as the leader. Did these situations feel different? What did you observe?

Little Critters

The Buddha taught that all life is precious and should be respected and loved. This activity helps us connect with the many small life-forms with whom we share our planet.

As you go into this activity, recall that *metta* means loving-kindness, or wishing that others be happy. As we observe the little critters going about their days, we can imagine their happiness and feel love and friendliness toward them.

Find a location outside in nature. Begin this activity with some mindful walking. Direct your attention to the ground as you take careful, slow steps. Observe the dirt, grass, leaves, branches, and anything else you see scattered on the Earth.

As you take in the various nature objects at your feet, begin scanning the ground for little critters: spiders, beetles, ants, caterpillars, worms, ladybugs, crickets, and any other small beings you might find.

It may take some patience to continue practicing mindful walking until you find a critter. For help with mindful walking, take a look at *Step-by-Step Walking Meditation* (page 6). If you start to feel frustrated or upset, take a few deep breaths and continue walking. You might also remember that little critters can be frightened by and hide from a big human like yourself, so they don't get stepped on by accident.

If you're able to find a little critter, pause in your walking. If you're not able to find a little critter, you can watch a squirrel or bird from afar, or observe a plant or other nature being.

Find a place to stand or sit near the little being. Be sure to give it plenty of space so as not to frighten it, and do not disturb it by trying to touch it or pick it up. Spend several minutes focusing carefully on the critter. Watch how it moves or does not move. Look at its colors and patterns. Can you see its legs, antenna, eyes, or wings?

If your critter is moving quickly, you can gently follow behind it on your feet, watching where it goes and what it does. What do you think it is feeling? Is it working on a task? Where might it live? Try to tune into the little critter's experience as you follow it.

When you lose track of your little critter, wish it goodbye and let it go. You can continue by finding another little being to follow and observe until you feel connected to all the little critters of the Earth.

Water Ripples

Water is an interesting tool that we can use to learn about how things change over time. Its flowing nature and mirror-like surface can show us many of the Buddha's teachings in action. This meditation helps us focus on the properties of water and what they can teach us about the nature of things.

This meditation can be practiced outdoors near a body of water such as a creek, river, puddle, or stream. It can also be practiced inside using a medium-sized bowl filled with water.

If outside, find several small pebbles; if indoors, gather some coins. Find a comfortable place to sit in front of the body of water. Begin by taking three deep breaths, in through the nose and out through the mouth.

Look carefully at the water. What do you observe? How do you feel as you observe it? Look at the way the liquid moves or sits still. Pay attention to both the surface of the water and its depths.

Now take one of your pebbles. Hold it mindfully in your hand and feel the surface of the stone. Next, gently drop the pebble into the water and observe what happens. What do you see? Focus all your attention on how the water reacts to the dropped pebble.

Keep your eyes on the water and continue watching its movement. Can you notice the moment when the water stops making ripples? Where did they go? What remains?

Repeat this meditation with many pebbles of different sizes. You might even try dropping two pebbles at once and seeing how their ripples interact. As you continue to gaze at the water ripples, remember that every action, no matter how small, has a much larger, rippling effect.

Shadow Tracing

The Buddha taught that every action has effects that follow it. When we are kind, others feel the effects of our kindness, and our hearts feel joyous. When we are angry, others feel the effects of our anger, and we might feel upset. We can understand this idea when we think about shadows, the dark shapes that follow us around and look like us.

This activity will help you see action and effect by tracing shadows. For this activity you will need paper, drawing materials, and a light source. If you have access to a large roll of butcher paper, you can use that to trace whole bodies. If not, small paper will do fine for tracing hand shapes and other objects.

If you are using butcher paper, ask a caregiver to help you tape a large sheet of paper to a wall. Set up your light source so that it is facing the paper taped to the wall. Then, ask a friend to stand in front of the light source, strike a pose, and then freeze like a statue. It's now your job to use drawing materials to trace the shadow of your friend onto the butcher paper. Be careful not to write on the wall.

If you are using regular paper, sit at a table and set up your light source, like a flashlight or candle, so that it is facing the paper. You can then either ask a friend to make a shape with their hands or set up a toy or other object in front of the light. Then, carefully trace the shadow of the hands or objects onto the paper. You might also try this outside on a sunny day, and can draw with sidewalk chalk if you are able.

When you've finished tracing, take a moment to observe the original person or object and compare it to your shadow trace. How are they similar? How are they different? Do not worry if your shadow trace is not perfect; like our shadows, sometimes the effects of our actions are not exactly what we expect them to be.

Duck, Duck, Dukkha ✎

This game, a variation on Duck, Duck, Goose, is for four or more people. It can be played outside, or inside in a room with lots of space for running around.

The Buddha taught that *dukkha* ("doo-kuh"), or all the discomfort of life, comes from *attachment*. Attachment is when we want or crave things that we don't have and think that what we do have is not enough. The Buddha taught that we overcome dukkha, ending all suffering, when we let go of our attachments.

Begin this game by sitting in a circle. Select one person to be the living being. The living being will walk around the outside of the circle, gently touching each person's head and saying, "Duck." They will then select one person, touch their head, and say, "Dukkha—the source of suffering is attachment." The person named as the dukkha will then chase the living being around the circle to try to tag them. The living being has two choices: they can run around the circle away from

the dukkha until they are back to the empty spot in the circle, or they can turn to face the dukkha.

If the living being chooses to run away from the dukkha and they make it back to the empty spot in the circle and sit down without getting tagged, then the dukkha becomes the living being. If the dukkha tags the living being, then the living being stays the living being, the dukkha rejoins the group, and the cycle continues . . .

If the living being chooses to turn and face the dukkha, they say, "No more! The end of dukkha is letting go of attachment." The dukkha is then transformed into peace by moving to the middle of the circle.

Continue the game until all but the final living being are in the middle of the circle, transformed from dukkha into peace.

Making Friends with Our Monsters ✎

This activity is designed to help us work through challenging emotions. We might go through this activity when we feel sad, angry, upset, annoyed, or down. Gather some paper and drawing materials, and find a quiet place to sit alone or with a caregiver.

Take a few moments to focus on your heart. You might place your hands over your heart or give yourself a big, loving hug.

Now, notice how your body feels. Do you notice any tightness? Maybe some jumpy energy? Or is there calm? Sleepiness? Pain? Take three deep breaths.

Next observe your thoughts and emotions. What is arising? Name the feelings that come up by speaking them out loud, one at a time.

Choose one of the feelings that you spoke out loud. This is the feeling you will take time to connect and make friends with. Begin by imagining: If this feeling was transformed into a sneaky monster, how would it look? What would it be like?

We are going to write a letter or draw a picture to this monster to communicate with it.

In your letter or picture, let the sneaky monster know how you feel when it is present. Be kind to the monster, and remember that it might have a reason for making us feel a certain way. You might even ask the monster why it is acting as it is, and listen to hear if it gives you an answer.

You might also thank the monster for doing its best to help you with something. Maybe it is making you sad to let you know that you need something. Maybe it is making you feel lonely to let you know you need to spend time with friends and family. Maybe it is making you angry to let you know there is a conflict that needs your attention.

Finally, offer the sneaky emotion monster the gift of friendship. You might write or draw an intention to be open to and accepting of the monster as it is, and not ask it to change. Sometimes, when we accept monsters as they are, some magical transformation occurs on its own!

Mandala Drawing

A *mandala* is a symbol in Buddhism that represents the universe where we live. Mandalas tend to be in the shape of a circle, but can sometimes be squares, too. They tend to be symmetrical, meaning they show a repeating pattern around the circle or square that looks the same on each side.

This activity is about creating mandala designs with others in order to connect with community, or *sangha*. You will need two or more people seated in a circle or across from one another, some sheets of paper, and drawing materials. While working through this activity, practice quiet focus as you enjoy the peace of mandala-drawing.

Each participant will begin with one piece of paper and draw the beginning of the mandala in the middle of the paper. This can be a circle or square, and may be made up of solid lines, dotted lines, shapes, or patterns. Keep this first design small; the mandala will grow as each participant has a chance to add to it.

When each participant has completed the first design, everyone will pass their papers to the left. Everyone will then add another layer of design to the mandala that the previous participant started. You can add lines, shapes, patterns, or any other creative design you can think of. Just make sure to repeat the patterns around the entire circle or square to keep the mandala symmetrical.

Continue passing the mandalas around the circle until the designs feel complete, and then take time to admire what the group created together.

Chapter 3

NIGHT

Phew, is anyone else feeling sleepy? It's almost that time to lie down to give our bodies and minds a rest. This chapter will help you transition from day to night. This is a special time for settling down, unwinding, processing, and letting go. The sun goes down, light turns to dark, and often the temperature cools off. You might also notice your body signaling to you that night is coming with heavy eyes, tired muscles, and deeper breathing. When you start to notice any of these signs, go ahead and choose the activity in this chapter that feels right for you. The activities and active meditations are best for after dinner, the stories are great for reading in bed, and the calmer meditations can be practiced as you fall asleep. All will help prepare you for a good night's sleep. Happy practicing, rest up, and sweet dreams.

Mara to Tea

This story is adapted from Buddhist mythology.

It is said that on the night the Buddha achieved enlightenment, he was tempted by a demon named Mara, the Evil One. Mara came to the Buddha while he was meditating and tried to stop him from awakening.

Mara brought the Buddha all kinds of distractions such as delicious food, beautiful brides for him to marry, and discouraging words. In this way Mara tried to make the Buddha feel greed, attachment, distraction, and self-doubt.

But the Buddha stayed concentrated on his meditation and did not give in to Mara, the Evil One, and thus the Buddha achieved enlightenment.

Now it is said that even after the Buddha awakened, Mara continued to make sneaky appearances before the Holy One. He would sneak up and try to catch the Buddha by surprise with anger and temptation.

The Buddha's cousin and loyal attendant Ananda always looked out for Mara on behalf of the Buddha, and would tell his master if he saw the Evil One coming.

Well, one such day, Ananda indeed spotted the Evil One making his way toward the Buddha. Ananda stood his ground at the Buddha's door and asked Mara what he wanted.

"I only wish to pay the great Buddha a visit," whispered the Evil One with malice. "Do let him know I'm here, Ananda."

Ananda hesitated. Part of his job was to protect the Buddha, and Mara could be very dangerous. But Ananda had also vowed to never tell a lie, and so he went to the Buddha and told him of his demon guest.

"Ah, Mara," replied the Buddha. "How wonderful! Invite him in please, Ananda."

And so Ananda, rather confused, obeyed his master and led Mara, the Evil One, into the Buddha's room. Ananda watched as the Buddha greeted the Evil One.

"Mara, my old friend! Welcome. Please, take a seat." And the Buddha offered the demon his most comfortable cushion. The Buddha then went to fetch his finest tea and poured the wholesome herbal drink for his guest. Only then did the Buddha take his own seat and tea.

Mara was flabbergasted by this warm welcome. He had expected that the Buddha would run away in fear. He had thought that the Buddha would shut the door in his face for all the evil he had done. And yet, here sat the Holy One, offering the Evil One the most gracious hospitality.

Mara tried to arouse anger or temptation over tea, but the Buddha was so welcoming and kind that all of Mara's evil was transformed and became harmless.

Eventually, Mara left. He was full of delicious tea, and his heart was softened by the great compassion and generosity of the Holy One.

And so may we all face the anger, temptation, distraction, and doubt of Mara that arises in all of our lives with the same welcoming kindness.

WHEN "MARA" APPEARS IN THE MIND IN THE FORM OF ANGER, GREED, DOUBT, OR DISTRACTION, WE SHOULD WELCOME THESE FEELINGS WITH KINDNESS. EVERYONE, EVEN GROWN-UPS, EXPERIENCES THESE FEELINGS, AND THEY ARE NATURAL. FEELING THESE FEELINGS DOES NOT MAKE US BAD. THIS DOES NOT MEAN WE SHOULD LET THEM TAKE OVER OUR ACTIONS, BUT IT MEANS WE DON'T PUSH THESE FEELINGS AWAY.

Gratitude Journal ✏️

Gratitude is a feeling you have when you are thankful or appreciative. You might feel gratitude for something you have, such as a home, food, or toy. You might also feel gratitude for someone you know, such as a parent, sibling, friend, pet, or teacher. When you feel gratitude, you are happy that you have something or know someone. You also know that your life would be very different if you did not have that thing or know that person.

This activity gives you a chance to reflect on all the wonderful things and people in your life at the end of the day. It is a wonderful way to grow your gratitude. This activity requires paper and drawing materials. If you'd like to do this activity every night, you might want to make your entries in a notebook or journal to keep them all in one place.

Begin by reflecting on your day today. What went well? Did you do something fun or silly? Did you eat something

delicious or play with a good friend? Think about the different things you did, the objects you used, and the people who were with you.

Now, imagine that one of the items or people you were with today—POOF—disappeared! How would your day be different? How would you feel?

Now remember your day again. Do you feel any *gratitude* or thankfulness for anyone or anything? This can be your gratitude journal entry for the day. Draw a picture or write about the things or people you feel grateful for and why you feel grateful for them. When you finish this activity, you might say "Thank you" out loud to yourself, or to a person you are grateful for, as an expression of your gratitude.

Forgiveness Frees Me

What does it mean to forgive someone? When you forgive someone, you let go of any anger or blame you feel toward them. Forgiveness is like telling someone, "It's alright. I know you made a mistake, and I also know you are a good person." Forgiveness helps us feel more at ease, feels good for others, and makes our friendships stronger.

This meditation helps us practice forgiveness in a fun way at the end of the day. It is a great practice if you had a disagreement or conflict with someone. This meditation requires a blanket.

Lay your blanket out flat on the floor or bed. Lie down on top of one end of the blanket and close your eyes. Take a moment to notice how the blanket feels beneath you. What is its texture? Is it warm or cool? Can you feel the floor or bed beneath it?

Next, think of a conflict you encountered today. Perhaps you disagreed with a friend at recess. Or maybe someone said unkind words to you. As you think of what happened, slowly begin to roll yourself up into the blanket. Keep your eyes closed, and focus on what happened as you roll.

Once you're all rolled up in the blanket, take a pause and notice how you feel. Can you move your arms or legs? How does your belly feel? You're probably wrapped up snug like a blanket burrito. You might roll around for a moment or two and explore how it feels to be in a blanket burrito.

Staying in your burrito, come back to a lying position and close your eyes again. Remember again the conflict that happened today. Do you feel angry or resentful of someone? Maybe hurt or confused? Who inspires these feelings in you?

Now, imagine this person's wonderful qualities. Maybe they are usually kind, or maybe they love their family a lot. Maybe they get along well with animals, or maybe they are a skilled artist.

As you reflect on this person's good qualities, imagine what it would be like to let go of the anger you are feeling towards them. Then, when you start to feel the anger slip away, begin to unroll yourself from your burrito blanket and say aloud, "I forgive you."

As you unroll yourself, you can stretch your arms and legs and feel the freedom of both your body and your heart as you practice forgiveness.

Clench and Let Go

Some days we experience stress and discomfort. This meditation helps us explore what that tension feels like in our bodies, and then let it sail away at the end of the day to help prepare for sleep.

Find a comfortable place to sit. You can sit on the floor, a cushion, chair, or bed. Begin by closing your eyes and thinking about anything that felt stressful or upsetting today. Perhaps you had a challenging moment with a friend, or maybe you felt distressed when a neighborhood dog barked at you. Think about anything that was difficult for you today, and say it out loud.

As you say what happened out loud, notice how your body feels. Do any of your muscles feel tense? If so, which ones? Does your breathing change at all? How do your eyes, forehead, and chest feel?

It might feel hard to stay focused on something challenging that happened, especially if you notice your body has a strong reaction. If it feels too hard, try talking about it with a caregiver and see if that helps. You can also try taking three deep belly breaths.

Next, hold your arms out straight in front of you and close your eyes. Once again think about the challenging moment that happened. As you do so, take a breath in and clench your fists as tight as you can. Squeeze your fingers together and feel all the muscles in your hand tighten as you recall what happened.

Then, breathe out nice and loud through your mouth and open your hands wide. Stretch your fingers out in all directions, and you might even shake your wrists. As you exhale and stretch your hands, imagine letting go of the challenge you faced today. You might imagine it floating away in the form of dark smoke, leaving through your hands and breath.

Repeat this meditation with as many challenging moments you faced today. You might even do it more than once with the same challenge, if it doesn't seem to want to be let go.

When you're finished clenching and letting go, close the meditation with three more deep belly breaths and a bow.

The Cold Porcupines

This story is adapted from a popular folktale.

It was the coldest winter the animals had ever seen. Icicles grew from their noses. They shivered all the way to their bones when the freezing wind blew.

Most of the animals huddled together in groups for warmth. They took turns sitting on the outside of the huddle and feeling most of the wind, so that no one stayed too cold for too long.

But the porcupines had a problem. Each time they tried to huddle together, they were poked and prodded by the sharp quills of their neighbors. They tried to position themselves just right so they would not get scratched, but it was an impossible task.

They decided to back away from each other.

But when they did so, they began to freeze. Their teeth chattered, their limbs grew numb, and they knew they needed warmth. One of the smallest porcupines spoke up, "My neighbors, if we do not huddle together for warmth we will surely freeze to death. It is true we will get some scratches and cuts from our quills, but these will heal with time. If we freeze, we will never have the chance to heal. Come, let us draw close together and cuddle for warmth."

And so the porcupines gathered round the wise little one. It is true they had some scratches, some cuts, and some pinches from the quills. But soon the weather began to warm, and the cold winter winds made way for a sunny spring. The porcupines' little wounds healed, and they had received the warmth of the closeness with their neighbors.

RELATIONSHIPS CAN SOMETIMES BE HARD, BUT THEY ARE ESSENTIAL TO OUR WELL-BEING AND GIVE OUR HEARTS WARMTH.

Mantra Meditation

If you like singing, humming, or making sounds, mantra meditation might be for you. A *mantra* is a group of words or sounds that are repeated again and again as a form of meditation. This is also called *chanting*. When we chant, we can enter a special state of concentration, and also feel the powerful energy of the words we say.

Some schools of Buddhism practice chanting more than others, and some chant words in the traditional Buddhist languages. The example offered here is in the ancient Indian language Sanskrit. You can practice mantra chanting using this example, another mantra you find elsewhere, or with your own mantra you make up yourself. For guidance on how to do that, check out the activity *My Very Om Mantra* (page 68).

Find a comfortable place to sit. Place your hands in your lap, resting on your legs, or covering your heart or belly. It can be nice to feel the vibrations in your chest while you chant. You can also choose to practice this meditation by yourself or with your family, caregiver, or friends. If you are able to do this meditation with others, notice how it feels to chant in a group.

When you're ready, close your eyes and begin by chanting the word "Om." Breathe in deeply through your nose, and when you've filled your lungs with as much air as you can, open your mouth wide in an "o" shape and make the sound "Om" as you breathe out. Keep making the "Om" sound until there is no more air left to breathe out. Repeat this two more times, and notice how your body feels.

Next, chant the following mantra: "Om Mani Padme Hum, Om Ma-ni Pad-me Hum, Om Mani Padme Hum."

This is the mantra of the Buddha of compassion. It means "praise to the jewel in the lotus flower" in Sanskrit. It reminds us that we have beautiful nature inside ourselves, like a jewel in a lotus flower that grows out of the mud.

Repeat this mantra three or more times and feel your heart fill with compassion as you chant. You might add more sounds on to the end of this mantra, or play with the different sounds already here. Take your time to feel how each word sounds vibrating in your body.

When you've finished chanting, say one more "Om" on a deep breath and close your practice with a bow.

My Very Om Mantra ✏️

Mantra chanting is a form of meditation that is great for people who love to sing, hum, whistle, drum, and make sounds. *Mantras* are words or sounds, such as "Om," that are repeated again and again. Mantras are often in traditional languages, but some are in English. This activity will help you to make up your very own mantra for chanting. If you'd like to learn a traditional Buddhist mantra, check out *Mantra Meditation* (page 66).

You don't need special materials for this activity, but if you'd like to write or draw out different ideas you have, you can use paper and drawing materials.

Begin by closing your eyes and placing your hands on your heart. How do you feel right now?

Do you notice anything in your body?

Are any emotions arising? What are they?

What is your mind thinking about?

Choose one thing that you notice, something about your body, emotions, or thoughts. Try describing it out loud to yourself. You can also draw or write about it. What is the sensation, emotion, or thought like? How is it to experience it?

Finally, look at your description or drawing. How can you make peace with the sensation, emotion, or thought? Is it perfect as it is? Can you relax with it? Accept it? Play with it?

The answer to this question will be your mantra. It might be one word, such as "Relax," "Accept," or "Play." It might be a phrase such as, "It is what it is," "It's perfect as it is," "I accept this," or "Here we are." Or it might just be a sound that feels good to you such as "Oooo," "Raaaa," or "Yeeeee."

Once you've selected your word, phrase, or sound, you have made your very own mantra. You can now practice mantra meditation with it by sitting with your eyes closed and chanting your mantra out loud again and again. Happy chanting.

Siddhartha's Story

This story is based on the life of the historical Buddha, Siddhartha Gautama.

Long, long ago in the year 500 BC in Nepal, a queen gave birth to a son and named him Siddhartha.

    Siddhartha was born a prince, and soon after his birth many visitors came to see the royal baby. Among those visitors was Asita, a great mystic and fortune-teller. As Asita held the baby prince, he had a vision. Prince Siddhartha would either become a powerful king or a wise spiritual teacher.

Siddhartha's father, the king, wanted his son to take over his kingdom. He thus hoped Prince Siddhartha would become a power king, not a wise spiritual teacher. So he decided to do everything to keep Prince Siddhartha content at the palaces.

As Prince Siddhartha grew up, he was given everything he could ever want. He had abundant food and sweets. He could play any game or sport he wanted. He had many friends and playmates. However, the king made sure that Siddhartha never saw human suffering. Siddhartha knew nothing about sickness, aging, or death.

Prince Siddhartha lived happily in his palaces until he was 29 years old, when he decided it was time to leave and meet the villagers. The king tried to stop Siddhartha, but the prince ventured out with his servant Channa.

While walking through one of the villages, Siddhartha came across a man who was very ill. "What is wrong with you, my friend?" asked Siddhartha.

"I am sick," said the man.

Siddhartha was confused. He did not know what "sick" meant, but it looked very unpleasant. "Channa, what is 'sick'?" Siddhartha asked.

Channa explained, "Sometimes the body catches a disease that causes harm to the physical form." Siddhartha hung his head in sadness upon hearing this, but continued walking.

Soon Siddhartha came across an old woman. He felt frightened by her wrinkles and hunchback. "What is wrong with you, my lady?" asked Siddhartha.

"I don't know what you mean," replied the old lady. "I am just old!"

Again, Siddhartha was confused. He did not know what "old" meant either. But it too looked unpleasant. Channa again explained: "Everyone grows old, my lord. As time passes, the body breaks down." Siddhartha shed a tear, but again continued walking.

Soon Siddhartha came across the morgue, where a corpse lay in a casket. "Channa, is this person sleeping? Why do they not breathe?"

"My lord, this is the body of someone who has died. They are no longer with us, only their body."

"Died?" asked Siddhartha.

"Yes, my lord," replied Channa. "It means to pass on out of this life. Every living being must die one day."

Siddhartha was shocked and shaken by these new discoveries. He returned to his palaces, but was no longer enjoying himself. He tried to enjoy his sweets and games, but he felt no joy. He decided to run away in search of true happiness.

Soon Siddhartha came across a group of holy people meditating in a forest. They invited Siddhartha to join them and explained that they ate only five grains of rice a day. "This will make you holy," they said. "It will purify your body and bring you true happiness."

Siddhartha agreed, and the holy people taught him how to meditate. Day after day Siddhartha sat in meditation, practicing from morning until night, eating only his five grains of rice a day.

Years passed, and Siddhartha felt that meditation was a very sacred and wonderful practice, but his body was weak with hunger. He left the forest and continued on his way. "I think meditation may indeed bring me to true happiness," he thought, "but I am too hungry to focus on my practice!"

One day Siddhartha came across a fig tree, and lay down to rest. His body was thin and frail, and he felt he could hardly move. Soon a young girl named Sujata noticed Siddhartha sitting under the tree. She fetched some rice pudding and offered it to the hungry stranger.

Siddhartha gratefully accepted the gift and joyfully ate all the rice pudding. Feeling stronger and more focused, he sat up and pronounced, "I will sit under this tree until I realize what leads to true happiness, and I will not move otherwise."

With this great determination and energy, Siddhartha entered a deep state of meditation.

He sat and sat, and sat some more, traveling ever deeper into his mind.

After a very long night, Siddhartha awakened under the fig tree, and became the Buddha.

At once he understood that suffering is part of life. He understood where suffering comes from. And he understood how to end suffering and find true happiness.

He began teaching his realizations as the Dharma, or teachings. And so began Buddhism.

TRUE HAPPINESS WILL NOT COME FROM HAVING TOO MUCH, OR TOO LITTLE, BUT BY PRACTICING BALANCE.

The Monkey Bridge

This is a retelling of a story from the Jataka Tales. The Jataka Tales are an ancient collection of imaginative stories about the Buddha as both a human and an animal.

You may recall, before the Buddha was born as a human, he was born as a Monkey Queen to a family of 80,000 monkeys. The Monkey Queen was wise and kind, and watched over her monkey family with love.

During the spring, the monkeys traveled to a forest by the Ganges River. In this season, the trees would sprout with delicious, sweet mangos, and the monkeys were joyous and grateful.

However, down the river was the human city of Varanasi. The wise Monkey Queen knew of the potential danger, so she warned her family:

"We must pluck every fruit that grows on the trees and never let a mango fall into the water. If it is carried downstream, the humans are sure to come take all the fruit, and we will have to flee for our lives."

The monkeys had great trust in their queen, so they were careful to never let a fruit fall into the river. But one day, a single small ripe fruit silently fell from the tree. It plopped into the river below and was carried down, down, down to Varanasi.

The little mango was rolling along the waves of the river while the King of Varanasi was bathing. The king plucked the fruit from the water, cut it open, and took a small taste. "This . . . is . . . the FINEST fruit I have ever tasted! I must go in search of the source of this fruit."

And with that, the King of Varanasi gathered a group and set up the river Ganges in search of the delicious fruit.

After many days of travel, the king and his retinue arrived at the forest of mango trees and spotted the brightly colored fruit hanging from the branches. "There!" shouted the king. But as they steered their ships closer, the king noticed little creatures scurrying around atop the branches and plucking the fruit from the trees.

"Monkeys?" he exclaimed. "They are eating my precious fruit. Surround them. They must not escape!"

The monkeys cried out in fear and looked to their queen. "Fear not, my family. Follow me!"

The queen ran to the end of a branch and tied a long, thick vine to her ankle. It was several hundred feet to the next tree, but the mighty queen stepped back and then ran forth and jumped mightily into the wind. She grasped the branch of the neighboring tree but, alas, the vine was too short. The queen hung in the air, her ankle tied to the vine and her arms stretched out to the tree branch.

"My family," she shouted. "Run over the vine and across my back to safety." The monkeys obeyed and ran over their leader's back. Her back became bruised and scratched, but she did not let go.

The King of Varanasi watched on as the selfless queen's back broke under the weight of her family members. The king's eyes filled with tears as he shouted, "Wait! See how this noble leader has sacrificed herself for her people. Help her down and get her water."

The King of Varanasi held the injured Monkey Queen in his arms. "You made your body into a bridge to save your family. You have sacrificed your body for your people. How can you give so much?"

The Monkey Queen smiled and said, "Serving my family brings me peace and joy. What happens to my single body does not matter to me. I only care that I may serve with love."

And the blessed Monkey Queen took her last breath and died in the king's arms. The king bowed his head humbly and said, "I have much to learn from this most noble queen." And with that, the King of Varanasi returned to his city and ruled over his people with kindness and love.

THIS STORY SHOWS THE BIGGEST SACRIFICE: ONE'S OWN LIFE. YET IN OUR DAY-TO-DAY LIVES WE HAVE TO GIVE UP SOMETHING OF OURSELVES ON A SMALLER SCALE IN ORDER TO SERVE OTHERS. SERVING OTHERS BRINGS PEACE AND JOY TO YOUR HEART.

The Tortoise and the Geese

This is a retelling of a story from the Jataka Tales. The Jataka Tales are an ancient collection of imaginative stories about the Buddha as both a human and an animal.

Once long ago there was an old tortoise and two friendly geese. The three animals lived together in a pond in the Himalayan mountains. Over the years they became good friends and spent their days playing about in the water.

One day, the geese invited the old tortoise to come visit their home on the other side of the mountains. "It is a most splendid place," they told the tortoise. "You must join us on our journey."

"Oh," replied the tortoise. "But I do not have wings. I cannot fly. And it would take much too long to cross the mountains by foot."

"Well," said the geese. "Can you keep your mouth shut and not speak?"

"Why yes," answered the tortoise. "That is no problem for me."

With that, the geese found a sturdy stick and held it out to the tortoise. "Hold on to the middle of this stick with your teeth and do not open your mouth. We will take each end in our beaks and fly side by side. That way, we will carry you to our home."

"How wonderful," exclaimed the tortoise. He grasped the stick with this mouth and off they flew together.

The tortoise was greatly enjoying the view when the animals flew over the city of Varanasi. Below in the city, many young children were out playing in the streets when they saw the strange trio of animals flying overhead.

"Look up there," cried one of the children. "A turtle being carried by geese. That is ridiculous." The children began laughing and pointing at the tortoise.

The tortoise tried to ignore their cruel laughs, but he felt anger arising in his chest.

"Ha," shouted the children. "That dumb turtle thinks it can fly!"

And with that, the old tortoise shouted back, "I'm not a turtle, and I'm not dumb!"

But of course, as soon as the tortoise opened his mouth to speak, he lost hold of the stick and began to fall down, down, down to the ground. Thump! The old tortoise landed in the garden of the king's palace, his shell cracked and his head very dizzy.

The king rushed out with his servants to see what had made the loud sound, and there he found the old tortoise. Now, it just so happens that the King of Varanasi was very talkative. He was kind at heart, but would chat and chat with everyone around him, never giving anyone else a chance to share.

"How did this tortoise fall from the sky?" asked the chatty king. "How did he even get up high enough to fall? Can he fly? I don't see any wings. The poor thing looks hurt."

The king's servants inspected the tortoise and looked up to see the geese flying overhead, still carrying the stick. "My Lord, it appears that the tortoise was flying with these geese, but could not resist opening his mouth to speak. And thus he fell."

The king paused in silence, then scooped up the old tortoise and carried him into the palace for care. From that day forward, the king was a little less talkative, and the tortoise also learned to be wiser with his speech.

IT IS IMPORTANT TO BE WISE WITH THE WORDS YOU SAY, INCLUDING WHEN YOU SAY THEM.

Rooms of the Heart

This is a great activity to wind down the evening with some reflection and art. It requires only paper and drawing materials.

Reflection: Take a moment to close your eyes and feel your heartspace—the part of your chest where your heart lives. You might gently place your hands over your heart and feel it beating. Now, imagine that your heart is a house. The house of your heart contains many rooms. In each room lives someone or something that you love. Perhaps one room is for your parents, and another room is for your dog. Maybe your favorite song lives in another room, and your favorite place in nature lives in another. Imagine walking through each room and discovering the things you love. As you explore, something amazing happens: with every room you find, the house gets bigger. You begin to see that you never run out of rooms in your heart for the ones you love.

Activity: Draw a large heart covering most of the paper. Divide the heart into sections of different shapes and sizes. In each section, draw or write the name of someone or something you love. Each section represents a room in your heart. As you fill in each room, feel what it's like to love whoever lives there. Spend a few moments with each room that you draw or label before moving on to the next one. When every section has been filled in, admire your full heart and all the love that is in it.

Good News, Bad News ◉

This story is adapted from a Chinese parable; it is a classic story that helps explain a big idea.

Once there was a humble Chinese farmer named Hui. Hui was very wise, and always maintained *equanimity*: evenness or mental steadiness. She knew that things that seemed like good news were not always good, and things that seemed like bad news were not always bad. Hui never reacted strongly to things that happened to her.

One day, Hui's horse ran away. Hui depended on her horse for maintaining her farm, so this seemed very unfortunate. Hui's neighbors expressed their condolences when they heard. "We are so sorry to hear about your horse. That is most unfortunate that she ran away."

"Maybe," Hui replied. "We'll see." She did not feel upset or worried, since she knew that what seemed like bad news did not always turn out to be bad.

To the neighbors' surprise, Hui's horse returned the next day and brought three wild mares with her. "Wow," exclaimed the neighbors. "Now you have four horses instead of just one. How lucky you are!"

"Maybe," said Hui. "We'll see." She did not become overly excited or smug about her new horses, since she knew that what seemed like good news did not always turn out to be good.

The next day, Hui's son Zhi went out to tame the wild horses. Zhi struggled to hang on while riding one of the wild mares, but was thrown to the ground and broke his leg. Hui rushed her son to the doctor, who expressed their apologies to Hui. "This is a very

bad break," they said. "I am sorry to deliver the unfortunate news that Zhi may walk with a limp for his whole life."

Zhi looked to his mother. "Oh, Mama, isn't that just awful?"

Hui patted her son on the back and smiled, "Maybe, my dear. But we'll see."

A week later, a government official came to town with an important announcement. China was at war, and all able-bodied men would be required to become soldiers. Zhi hobbled out on his crutches and looked at his mother. "Mama, I suppose you were right. It was not such bad news after all that I have this injury. If I were able-bodied, then I would be leaving to go fight in the war, and I might never have returned. I suppose it was good news after all."

Hui smiled calmly at her son and said, "Maybe. We'll see."

THINGS THAT SEEM LIKE BAD NEWS, SOMETIMES LEAD TO GOOD THINGS. THINGS THAT SEEM LIKE GOOD NEWS, SOMETIMES LEAD TO BAD THINGS. WHILE IT IS NATURAL TO REJOICE WHEN SOMETHING WONDERFUL HAPPENS, AND CRY WHEN SOMETHING SAD HAPPENS, REMEMBER THAT THERE'S ALWAYS SOMETHING ELSE JUST AROUND THE CORNER, AND IT MIGHT NOT BE WHAT YOU THINK.

Spaghetti Wiggle Relaxation

Ah, so you're all settled into bed and it's almost time to drift off to sleep. But sometimes our bodies need a little help relaxing. This meditation will help you get the last of the wiggles out to get your body ready for sleep.

To begin this meditation, lie on your back in bed. Lay your hands by your side, facing up. Let your feet fall open. Now, focus on one of your arms, and imagine it is a piece of spaghetti. Beginning with your fingers, bring some small wiggles to your spaghetti arm. Move up through your hand, forearm, upper arm, and shoulder. Wiggle that spaghetti arm until there are no more wiggles left.

When you're all done shaking your spaghetti arm, lift it up high and then let it drop onto the bed. Hold it very still and see how it feels. Repeat this spaghetti-wiggling business with your other arm.

Once you've wiggled out both of your arms and they are lying totally still on the bed, focus on one of your legs, and imagine that it, too,

is a piece of spaghetti. Begin by wiggling your toes, then rotating your ankle, then your knee, thigh, and then your whole leg. Shake that spaghetti leg until there's no more wiggles left. Then, lift your leg up as high as you can, and let it drop onto the bed and become very, very still. Repeat with your other leg as well.

When both your spaghetti arms and spaghetti legs have been wiggled out, they should all be lying very still on the bed. Notice how they feel. Close this relaxation meditation with three deep breaths.

The Golden Goose

This is a retelling of a story from the Jataka Tales. The Jataka Tales are an ancient collection of imaginative stories about the Buddha as both a human and an animal.

Once long ago there lived a father, mother, daughter, and son. The family was very poor and rarely had enough to eat.

One day, the father decided it was time he traveled to the city to seek his fortune. He planned to work until he made enough money to feed his family for the winter and then return home.

However, after only a couple of hours of traveling, the father came across a magical fairy in the woods. "What are you seeking, traveler?" she asked the man.

"Oh, kind fairy, I seek riches so that I might feed my poor family."

"Why, is that all?" cried the fairy. And with a swish of her wrist, the little winged creature put a spell on the man. He turned into a goose.

The fairy disappeared in a cloud of purple, sparkling smoke, and the goose flew off to a pond. "What am I to do?" thought the goose. "How am I to feed my family now?"

But as the goose approached the pond, he noticed his reflection and saw that his feathers were made of gold. "I am not just any goose. I am a golden goose!"

And so the goose made his way back to the family's home. The goose was greeted by the mother and two children.

"Sweet family, see here that my feathers are made of pure, precious gold. I know you are poor and need money to pay for food." The goose plucked one of its feathers from its body and handed it to the mother. "Take this golden feather and sell it at the market. It should earn you enough food for the week. Next week I will return with another feather, and thus you will never go hungry again."

The mother took the feather as the goose flew away. The next day the family made their way to the village and sold the golden feather, and they rejoiced in their good fortune.

The next week, the golden goose indeed returned and offered another feather. The children received it with gratitude and brought the offering to their mother.

But the mother became fearful and greedy, and made a plan to capture the golden goose and all of its fine feathers. She shared her plan with her children. "Next week when the golden goose returns, we shall capture it and pluck all of its feathers and sell them for a fortune. And then we shall keep it locked up and take each of its feathers as it grows. We will be very rich for the rest of our lives."

The children cried out in sorrow for the goose, but felt there was nothing they could do.

Sure enough, the next week the golden goose returned. And when he did, the mother trapped the bird and promptly plucked all its feathers.

The poor old goose lay in a cage in the corner, sore and naked, and he began to weep.

Over time, the goose's feathers began to grow back, but instead of the beautiful golden feathers, they grew back as the plain, white feathers of an ordinary goose. The fairy had ensured that if anyone took advantage of the bird, his feathers would no longer grow gold.

And so the greedy mother released the goose. He flew back to the pond and lived out his days happily among other birds. The children grew up wary of the dangers of greed.

GREED LEADS TO HARM BOTH FOR A PERSON WHO ACTS OUT OF GREED AND FOR THOSE AROUND THEM.

Pointing to the Moon

This story is adapted from a Zen Buddhist saying.

It is said that teachers are beings who transmit to us teachings.

It is said that teachings tell us how to find Truth.

It is said that Truth can only be found inside ourselves.

Truth is the knowing that the Buddha realized when he awakened.

And so there once was a very old wise teacher, Hekima, who tried to explain this to a group of her students. The group gathered one evening outside the temple for their lesson.

"My dear students, I am serving in the role of teacher, and I've come this evening to share with you a teaching that will lead you to Truth."

Hekima's students listened carefully to their teacher, eager to learn more Truth.

Hekima continued. "I will now point my hand just so. Tell me what you see."

The students looked at their teacher quite puzzled, then began to speak up one at a time. "I see your fingers," said one student.

"I see the palm of your hand," said another.

"Well, I notice your fingernails," one student chimed in.

"Keep observing," instructed Hekima.

"I see the back of your hand," offered another student.

"How about the finger that is pointing?" asked another.

"Ah," said Hekima. "And to what does it point?"

The students paused before slowly looking to where their teacher's finger pointed.

"The moon," exclaimed one student. "You finger is pointing to the moon!"

Hekima nodded. "My hand is like the teachings I give you. And the moon is like the Truth. Do not look only at the teachings, but to where they point you. I invite you to gaze at the Truth as you now gaze at the moon."

The students spent some time gazing at the moon as they pondered the words of their teacher. One student then asked, "So, when you teach us about kindness, we should not just think about kindness, we should practice being kind?"

And with that, Hekima bowed to her students and said, "That is how you will come to know Truth."

TEACHERS CAN SHOW US THE TEACHINGS AND HELP US TO UNDERSTAND, BUT WE HAVE TO DISCOVER THE TRUTH FOR OURSELVES THROUGH OUR OWN EXPERIENCES.

Bedtime Prayers for Peace

The end of a day, like the end of a practice, is a very special time for making wishes, dedications, or prayers for yourself and others. In some Buddhist traditions, it is believed that prayer has great power to heal and bestow peace. This meditation is great for experimenting with the magic of Buddhist prayer before bedtime.

Find a comfortable place to sit or lie down. You can also do this meditation once you're already tucked into bed. Place your hands over your heart and close your eyes. Take a moment to remember the magic that lives within a kind, heartfelt wish. Such wishes have a special transformative power to affect both yourself and others.

Now, is there someone in your life who needs some help and love right now? Maybe a friend, sibling, neighbor, caregiver, or you? Or maybe a group of people or animals need help, such as a family going through a hard time, or all the children without parents, or all the pets without homes. Hold this being or beings in your mind and in your heart.

Now, make a special wish or prayer for this being. How would you like for them to feel? Can you imagine them feeling this way? You might also say aloud or to yourself, "May you be happy. May you be free from pain. May you be peaceful."

Continue to make special prayers and wishes for everyone in your life, or the whole world, who you think need help. And remember, the more you believe in the power of your wishes, the more power they will have. May you be peaceful.

Drifting Off

Yaaawwwnnn . . . it's time for sleeping. And sometimes a meditation is helpful for the transition from being awake to being asleep. If you're trying to fall asleep and are sick of counting sheep, try this meditation instead.

Before beginning this meditation, make sure that you're all washed up, teeth brushed, and ready for sleeping. You might also want to dim or shut off the lights. The meditation will usually end with you falling asleep. Lie on your back in bed in a way that feels comfortable to you. You might have your arms lying out at your sides, or maybe resting on your belly.

When you're ready to begin, gently close your eyes and take a deep breath in through your nose and out through your mouth.

Now, imagine there is a butterfly or moth resting somewhere nearby. Maybe it is resting on your belly or chest, or maybe it is keeping its own space on your night table or beside you on the bed.

Picture the beautiful wings of the creature. Imagine their color, shape, and patterns. Perhaps they sparkle or glimmer, or maybe they are simpler.

Now, imagine the butterfly begins to flap its wings very slowly. You watch as its wings rise up and close together, then fall open, again, and again.

Soon you notice that the wings are flapping with your breathing. As you breathe in, the butterfly lifts its wings and they come together. As you breathe out, the wings fall open. And so you continue breathing, and so the butterfly's wings move up, and down, up, and down, up and down, up and down, as you drift off to sleep.

Resources

Sitting Together: A Family-Centered Curriculum on Mindfulness, Meditation, and Buddhist Teachings by Sumi Loundon Kim

This curriculum is made up of three books: a children's lesson book, an adult study guide, and an activity book. This wise and unique compendium offers comprehensive lessons on a wide range of Buddhist topics. Children's lessons correspond to adult teachings, so that children and parents can learn together at their own levels.

Mindfulfamilies.net

The material on this website was compiled by the author of *Sitting Together*, Sumi Loundon Kim. It includes information on mindful parenting, links to Buddhist music, and lists of additional resources. It also has a directory of Buddhist and mindfulness programs for family, children, and teens, organized by location.

Headspace / Headspace for Kids

This popular meditation app now includes in their subscription *Headspace for Kids*, a series of breathing exercises, activities, and meditations designed just for children. There are five themes for kids to choose from: calm, focus, kindness, sleep, and wake up. Meditations are grouped by age-appropriateness, up to age 12.

Betsy Rose music

Betsy Rose makes beautiful Buddhist-inspired folk music great for all ages. Her album *Calm Down Boogie* is especially kid-friendly, fun, and great for bedtime, and her album *In My Two Hands* is based on the teachings of Thich Nhat Hanh. Her music is available for listening on Spotify, YouTube, and her website, *betsyrosemusic.org.*

Stories by Jon J. Muth

Zen Shorts and its many sequels are beautifully illustrated books containing stories told by a giant panda named Stillwater. Each story conveys to children lessons relevant to Buddhism and ethics. Muth also authored *The Three Questions*, a kid-friendly adaptation of the Leo Tolstoy short story by the same name.

Buddhist Insight Network (BIN)

For those practicing in the Western Insight tradition, BIN is a great resource for finding a sangha near you (buddhistinsightnetwork.org/Sanghas). You can also specifically search for communities with a family program. The site also includes a retreat database and additional resources for growing your practice.

Index

About the Author

EMILY GRIFFITH BURKE is a Buddhist practitioner and teacher in Durham, North Carolina. She began her practice in Mahayana Tibetan Buddhism and now practices with the Theravada-based Insight tradition. Emily serves as a guest teacher with the Triangle Insight Meditation Community, Sati School teacher with the Mindful Families of Durham, and counselor with Kadampa Family Dharma Camp. Emily delights in serving her spiritual communities in a teaching role, and is grateful for every opportunity to engage with the practice.

In addition to her teaching roles, Emily serves as administrator of her young adults Kalyana Mitta (spiritual friendship) group, and is active in her Racial Affinity Group (Ruth King's model), and Engaged Buddhism Sangha. She has previously served on the Board of Directors of Triangle Insight Meditation Community.

Emily also enjoys activism, playing music, writing, reading, cooking, and playing board games with friends. You can find Emily at ThePracticingHuman.com.

EMILY'S FAVORITES:

GAME: Sushi Go!

ANIMAL: Cat

MEDITATION: Metta

BUDDHA: Green Tara

FOOD: Rice & Broccoli with Teriyaki Sauce

BUDDHIST TEACHER: Tara Brach

About the Illustrator

APRIL HARTMANN spent her childhood creating. She loved to draw and paint, but also sewed clothes for her stuffed toys, and even constructed furniture for them with scraps of wood. Today she combines drawing, painting, textures to create her art. She studied at the College for Creative Studies in Detroit and currently lives in Pennsylvania.